Who eats who in Grasslands?

Moira Butterfield

W

FRANKLIN WATTS
LONDON · SYDNEY

Designer: Cali Roberts
Editor: Robert Snedden
Art Director: Peter Scoulding
Editor-in-Chief: John C. Miles
Picture Research: Diana Morris
Artwork: Ian Thompson

First published in 2005
by Franklin Watts
96 Leonard Street
London
EC2A 4XD

Franklin Watts Australia
Level 17/207 Kent Street,
Sydney
NSW 2000

ISBN 0 7496 6081 3

Dewey classification number: 577.4

A CIP catalogue record for this book is
available from the British Library.

Printed in Malaysia

Note to parents and teachers
Every effort has been made by the Publishers to ensure
that the websites in this book are suitable for children,
that they are of the highest educational value, and that
they contain no inappropriate or offensive material.
However, because of the nature of the Internet, it is
impossible to guarantee that the contents of these sites
will not be altered. We strongly advise that Internet
access is supervised by a responsible adult.

Contents

Eat or be eaten!

All living things need energy to survive. Each day, plants and animals must get enough food to give them the energy they need to carry on living.

Food chains

Animals spend a lot of their time either looking for food or trying to avoid being eaten themselves. A list of who eats who can be linked together to make a food chain.

A simple food chain will usually begin with a plant, because plants can make their own food (see page 7). The first link in the chain will be to an animal that eats the plant. The next link will be to another animal that eats the plant-eater.

Plant-eating animals such as zebras are second in a grassland food chain.

(see page 7)

Yummy!

Some animals are scavengers, which means they eat the remains of dead creatures and plants. Scavenging animals find lots of food in grassland regions.

The lion is a top African grassland predator. It will hunt and eat grazing animals such as zebra.

Who Eats Who?

1. Plant (such as grass)

2. Herbivore (plant-eating animal such as a gazelle)

3. Carnivore (meat-eating animal such as a lion)

We're in the chain!

Humans are omnivores, which means we eat both plants and animals. We are the top predators in many food chains, including some grassland chains.

Food chain words

An animal that eats plants is called a herbivore. An animal that eats other animals is called a carnivore. An animal that eats both is called an omnivore. An animal that hunts and kills other creatures is also called a predator. The last link in a food chain is usually to a top predator, an animal so powerful that it has nothing to fear from any other creature.

Grassland habitat

The Earth has many different natural regions. These regions are called habitats. A habitat, such as a grassland, together with all the plants and animals suited to life there, forms an ecosystem. The plants and animals that live on the grasslands have to be able to cope with the conditions there.

Starting the chain

Because plants can make their own food they are at the start of almost every food chain. Grass is by far the most common plant in grassland regions.

Food for all

Many grassland creatures graze on plants and are in turn eaten by other animals. Without the plants at the start of the food chain, the animals at the end of the food chain would not survive, even though they might not eat plants themselves. Their prey would starve, so they in turn would die.

We're in the chain!

Some temperate grasslands make good grazing land for farm animals.

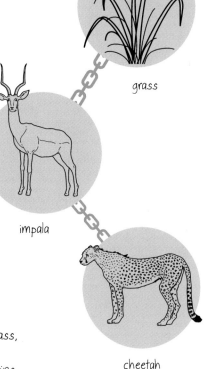

Who Eats Who?

grass

impala

cheetah

Plants, such as grass, are the basis of nearly all food chains.

A giraffe grazes on an acacia tree, a low-growing tree in the African savanna.

Sunlight starter

A plant can make its own food. It uses chemicals absorbed from its surroundings, plus energy captured from sunlight, to make sugar, which it uses to supply its energy needs. This process is called photosynthesis. Inside plant cells there is a substance called chlorophyll. This absorbs the sunlight needed to make sugar.

The plant menu

There are around 10,000 different types of grass in the world. The mix of grass plants growing on grassland varies according to the climate and the season.

On some grasslands, such as the African savanna, there are also low-growing trees and shrubs on which animals graze.

Chains to webs

Because plants are eaten by many different animals, and animals eat and are eaten by a variety of other animals, they can appear in more than one food chain. All the different food chains in a habitat can be woven together to form a food web. The food web shows the feeding links between plants and animals across the whole habitat.

Eating grass

Grass is unique in the plant world because, unlike other plants, it grows from the base, not from the tip. This means that, even though grass may be constantly grazed, it will continue to grow as long as the roots are undamaged.

A topi enjoys a meal of juicy grass stems.

After you...

Different grassland animals like to eat different parts of the grass stem. In the African savanna the topi, a type of antelope, uses its long, narrow mouth to feed on the long stems. Topi need to keep ahead of the wildebeest, whose wide, square mouths crop the grass short. Thompson's gazelles follow the wildebeest and nibble the delicate new shoots that appear after the wildebeest have had their share.

We're in the chain!

Cows make milk from the grass they eat. Humans collect the milk to drink.

Chewy food

Grass is a tough food to chew. A grass-eater's teeth are constantly being worn down by all the chewing. To combat this, grass-eating animals have teeth with open roots, which means their teeth keep on growing throughout their lives.

Yummy!

A ruminant's second stomach, the reticulum, is sometimes eaten by humans as a dish called tripe.

Multi-stomach

Grass is also hard to digest, so grazing animals need a bit of help. Ruminants, such as cattle, have four-compartment stomachs, each part containing micro-organisms that help break down the grass to release its nutrients. A cow sometimes brings the grass back up again from the first part of its stomach, called the rumen, for another chew (called 'chewing the cud'), before re-swallowing it.

Cattle graze on fertile grasslands in Hungary.

Tropical eating

The tropical grasslands of the world are permanently warm, but they do have wet and dry seasons, which affect the way animals find food.

A crocodile lurks by an African river to grab migrating wildebeest.

On the move

In the hot dry season the sun bakes the earth dry. The grass roots stay protected beneath the ground and when the wet season rains arrive they sprout again. The wet season rainfall varies over the savanna of east Africa, and large herds of wildebeest follow the rains to find new grass shoots. Wildebeest on the move are always wary of predators such as lions and hunting dogs that may be nearby. They are most nervous when crossing rivers as crocodiles can lurk under the water waiting to snatch a wildebeest as it wades across to the other side.

Grassy nurseries

Everything changes when the rainy season comes. The grasses grow rapidly, and more grass means more food for the animals to eat. Plant-eaters like the wildebeest time the births of their calves to occur when the grass is lushest. With so much grass to eat the females can produce plenty of milk for their young. Lions and other animals that hunt the plant-eaters have their cubs at this time too.

Who Eats Who?

Aquatic plants in the wet season / grass in the dry season

capybara

anaconda

Snake snack!

In the wet season, the flat grassy plains of the llanos in South America are flooded. The llanos is home to the world's biggest rodent, the capybara. They are able to swim and graze on aquatic plants that grow in the floodwater. But, swimming unseen beneath the surface, there may be a huge and hungry anaconda snake ready to wrap itself around a capybara and trap it in its muscular coils before swallowing it whole. In the dry season the anaconda will hide in the mud of a dried-up pool bed.

A family of capybara.

Yummy!

An anaconda can unhinge its jaw to swallow a whole capybara, which could be the size of a pig.

Temperate toughness

Temperate grasslands also have seasons, but they bring a different set of problems for the animals that live there. The summers may be very warm, but the winters can be bitterly cold with lots of snow.

Snow survival

In temperate grasslands it rains regularly throughout the year. In spring, summer and autumn there is plenty of good grazing for grass-eating animals, so plenty of good eating for the hunters, too. But they must all eat as much as they can to fatten themselves up before winter arrives, when plants die off, and food gets much harder to find.

Yummy!

A prairie rattlesnake injects its prey with venom, then lets it go and follows it until it dies. That way it is less trouble for the snake to swallow.

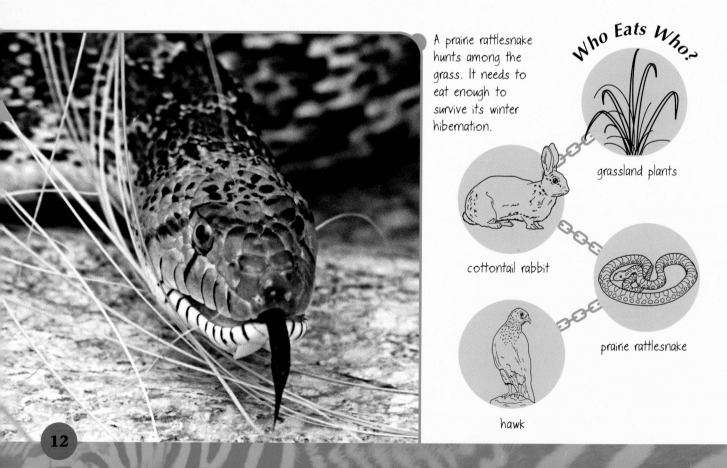

A prairie rattlesnake hunts among the grass. It needs to eat enough to survive its winter hibernation.

Who Eats Who?

grassland plants

cottontail rabbit

prairie rattlesnake

hawk

Hibernation

Some animals hibernate during winter. They become inactive and their heart rate and breathing slow right down. They don't eat at all during this time. Reptiles rely on the sun to keep warm, so when it gets cold in winter they survive by hibernating. For instance, the American prairie rattlesnake eats as many rodents and rabbits as it can during warm months, then crawls into an underground burrow to hibernate during the cold months. Its heart rate slows so that it only needs to use very small amounts of energy to stay alive while it hibernates.

Hairy help

Some animals brave the winter months, and carry on looking for food. For instance, the American bison has a thick hairy coat that keeps it warm, and a layer of fat to help sustain it in winter. It has large, broad feet to stop it from sinking into the snow as it moves in search of food, and it can use its enormous head like a bulldozer to reach grass under the snow.

We're in the chain!

Humans living in temperate climates used to gather and store as much food as possible in the autumn, salting meat to keep it edible over the winter.

An American bison finds grass to eat after a winter snowstorm.

Savanna hunters

The big cats of the African grasslands are top predators. They are strong and quick, with ferociously sharp teeth and claws. But not every hunt is successful, and sometimes they go hungry.

We're in the chain!

Lions and leopards will eat humans.

Masters of teamwork

Lions live in groups called prides. Hunting is led by the lionesses of the pride. One group creeps up behind a herd while another group moves into position ahead of them. When the trap is set, the first group of lionesses drives the herd towards the second. One animal, perhaps weaker or slower than the others, will be identified as the prey and the pride will chase it down and overwhelm it.

A group of lionesses kills a wildebeest.

Masters of stealth

Leopards are solitary hunters. They use their excellent night vision to track down their prey in the dark. A leopard will creep up stealthily on its prey. When it is close enough, it will launch an ambush and kill its victim with a bite from its powerful jaws. Leopards are so strong that they can drag their kill into a tree in order to feed undisturbed.

Masters of speed

The cheetah is the fastest grassland predator, and the fastest land animal on Earth. It hunts by using stealth and then speed. It can run in bursts of up to 110 km/h. It cannot keep up that speed for very long, so before it rushes at its prey it must creep as close as possible.

Yummy!

Big cats have rough tongues which they use to lick the hair off prey before biting into it.

Who Eats Who?

A cheetah chases gazelles. Gazelles can also run fast, so the cheetah must get as close as it can before beginning its ambush.

grass

Thompson's gazelle

cheetah

How to escape

The herds of grazing animals roaming the African savanna look like easy prey for any predator. But these apparently defenceless animals have a number of ways of making life difficult for their hungry enemies.

Camouflage

Many grassland animals have markings that help them to blend into the background. This is particularly true of grassland insects. For instance, the leafhopper insect looks just like part of the plant on which it feeds.

This leafhopper looks just like part of the flower on which it perches, confusing predators.

Who Eats Who?

sap of plant stalk

leafhopper

gecko lizard

Stripey disguise

A zebra's markings look obvious to us, but lions are colour-blind, so to them the zebra's stripes are hard to distinguish against the tall waving grasses. In a big herd it is hard for lions to pick out one zebra from another.

Safety in numbers

The sheer size of some herds makes it difficult for predators to identify and stalk one animal, particularly when the herd is on the move. It is made even harder for the hunters because grazers have acute senses that enable them to see, hear or smell predators from a long way off. Even if most members of the herd are grazing with their heads down, some at least will be alert and can sound a warning if danger approaches.

Yummy!

Most wildebeest give birth in the morning so that their calves can run by nightfall, when predators are most likely to attack them.

All born together

Young animals are particularly vulnerable to predators. Herds of grazing animals such as wildebeest synchronise the birth of their young, so they are all born at roughly the same time. That way, though some are bound to be taken by hunters, many of them will survive to adulthood.

A wary zebra watches a lioness crouching in the grass.

Clearing up

Nothing goes to waste in nature, even when plants and animals die. There is a whole group of animals that feast on dead flesh and plants. They are called scavengers.

Greedy gliders

Vultures are one of the most widespread bird scavengers on the grasslands. They feed on the carcasses of dead animals, which they pull apart with their strong necks and ferocious, sharp beaks. Although they are ungainly on the ground they can glide effortlessly on air currents high in the sky. They have good eyesight and a very keen sense of smell and can detect a dead or dying animal from a long way away.

A flock of vultures and a hyena look for dead food.

grass

droppings of grass-eating
animal such as eland

dung beetle

insect-eating bird
such as ibis

Dung delight

Grazing animals drop huge quantities of
dung across the grasslands every day. This is
recycled into the food chain by tiny bacteria
that break up the dung, releasing nutrients
back into the soil to fertilise the grass.
Meanwhile, the dung beetle has its own
way of recycling animal droppings. It rolls
up a small piece of dung and pushes it to a
suitable spot. Then it lays an egg in the
dung ball and buries it. When the beetle
larva hatches, its first meal will be the
nutritious parts of the dung.

Yummy!

Adult dung beetles
feed on the liquid
in dung. They
have special
mouthparts to
squeeze it out.

Hungry hyenas

African hyenas are vicious hunters and they are
also expert scavengers. They are persistent and,
working in a pack, they can even drive a lion
away from a kill by threatening it. They have
powerful jaws that can bite through and crunch
bone, and they have efficient digestive systems
that dissolve and digest bones, horns, hooves
and teeth within 24 hours.

Even a lion will
think twice about
taking on a pack
of hyenas.

Life on the prairie

The prairie is an enormous grassland that stretches across the centre of the USA and Canada. It is a temperate grassland, warm and dry in summer, but very cold in winter.

Grassland town-dweller

One of the most numerous animals on the prairie is the prairie dog, which is actually a type of ground-squirrel. It lives in a complex of underground burrows, often called a town. Some of these towns can house thousands of animals.

Prairie dogs eat plants and insects, and are always on guard for prairie predators such as eagles, hawks, snakes and coyotes. The entrance to a prairie dog burrow is raised above the ground. This helps to protect it from flooding and provides a good look-out perch.

A prairie dog looks out from a burrow entrance.

Who Eats Who?

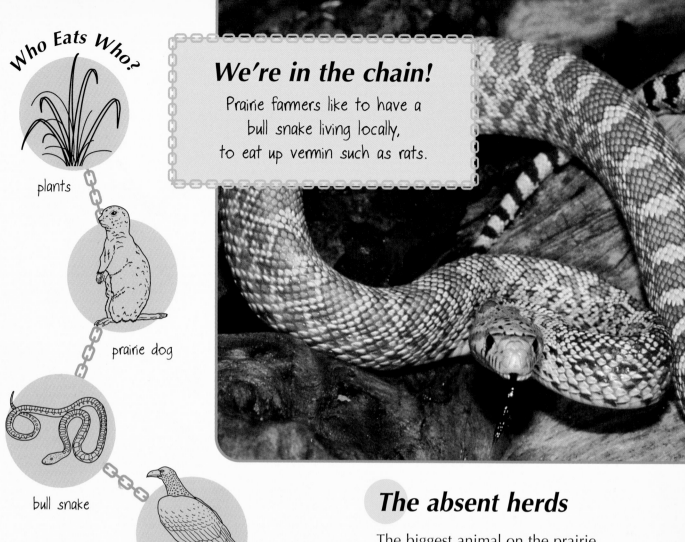

plants

prairie dog

bull snake

golden eagle

Reptile predator

Snakes prowl the grasslands looking for small animals to eat. The 1.5-m long bull snake hunts the prairie. Like all snakes it flicks its tongue in and out to collect smells as it travels along. Bull snakes suffocate their prey by squeezing it to death, then they swallow it whole. They can digest every part of their meal apart from fur or feathers. If a bull snake eats a large item of prey it won't need to eat again for several days.

The absent herds

The biggest animal on the prairie is the American bison (see page 13). It is a docile herbivore, but if cornered it will charge to defend itself and can run at up to 50 km/h. The prairie used to be home to huge herds of bison, but they were largely killed off by humans in the 1800s for their skins and meat. Now small herds are found in national parks and reserves.

Yummy!

If water supplies are frozen,
bison will eat snow.

Life on the pampas

The South America pampas grasslands stretch for thousands of kilometres between the Atlantic and the Andes mountains. It is flat and very fertile, and contains unique grassland wildlife.

Tiny chewers

Giant termite mounds up to 8 m high dot the pampas. The termites in a colony build the mounds with tiny pellets made from chewed-up mud and saliva. Termites eat plant remains, mostly in the form of wood. Like the grass-eating herbivores they need some help to digest it. Tiny micro-organisms live in the termite's gut and break down the wood so the termite can get some nourishment from it. The real work of digestion is done by bacteria that live inside the microbes that live inside the termites!

Yummy!

An anteater might eat up to 30,000 termites in a single day.

An anteater looks for a meal in a pampas termite nest built among branches.

Termite terminator

Termites are not safe inside their mighty mounds. The giant anteater is out to eat them. It uses its powerful forelegs and claws to break through the rock-hard mound. Then it sticks its long, narrow snout through the hole and shoots its 60-cm long, thin sticky whip-like tongue quickly in and out to slurp up the unlucky termites.

A Patagonian cavy keeps a watchful eye on the pampas.

Grazers and hunters

Plant-eating pampas rodents such as cavies feed while trying to avoid predators such as the vicious caracara hawk. The hawk's long legs and flat claws enable it to walk around hunting for food. It holds its prey down with one foot, while ripping it up with its sharp beak.

The biggest wild grazer on the pampas is a huge flightless bird called the rhea. It grows up to 1.5m tall, and will eat insects, lizards and plants.

Life on the steppe

The Eurasian steppe is the largest grassland in the world. It stretches from the borders of eastern Europe across Asia to Mongolia. It is hot and dry in summer but bitterly cold in winter, with temperatures falling to more than -20° C in places, so low it is hard for animals to survive.

A saiga's nose helps it survive the winter cold on the steppe by warming the air it breathes in.

Hairy big-nose

Saiga antelope graze the steppe. Huge herds of them migrate north in summer, and return to the warmer southern steppe in winter. The saiga's most prominent feature is its big nose, a complex structure of bones and chambers that helps to filter out dust in summer, and to warm up the freezing-cold air the saiga breathes in winter.

Saiga have a dual-layer coat. Coarse hair on the outside covers a softer, woolly undercoat that keeps the animal warm.

We're in the chain!

The steppes have rich black soil and plentiful rain so vast areas of it have been turned into farmland to grow cereal crops such as wheat, which is actually a type of grass.

A lone wolf on the snowy steppe.

Pack predator

Wolves hunt in packs across the steppe. They will eat anything that they can find, but like fresh meat best. They are not particularly fast, but they have lots of stamina and will chase a weak or young prey animal until it is so exhausted they can close in for the kill. Wolf pups are weaned off milk and on to meat early in their lives. When a parent comes home from a hunt, the pups lick its mouth until it regurgitates meat for them to eat.

Eye in the sky

In the drier areas of the steppe, there are lots of small rodents such as mice, gerbils and hamsters. They attract the attentions of predators, such as the rare and beautiful steppe eagle, a summer visitor. Birds of prey such as eagles and hawks have very good eyesight, and can spot a small animal rustling around in the grass from high up in the sky.

Who Eats Who?

plants

mouse

bird of prey such as steppe eagle

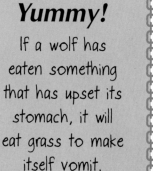

Yummy!

If a wolf has eaten something that has upset its stomach, it will eat grass to make itself vomit.

Grasslands in danger

Humans have had a big effect on grasslands for centuries. Now they are amongst the most endangered natural habitats in the world.

Grasslands become farms

The single biggest threat to grasslands is the expansion of farming. This can destroy the habitat of native animals. For instance, in South America, large areas of the pampas have been given over to farms. There is now much less space for native wild animals to graze, and so there is less food for wild predators, too.

Yummy!

Farm fertilisers carelessly spread by grassland farmers can poison wild animals, who unwittingly digest it when they eat plants or drink from rivers.

Much of what was once wild pampas is now used for cattle ranching, producing beef for customers around the world.

Human versus animal

Big dangerous predators are very unwelcome in grassland areas where humans live, and many have been hunted and killed. For instance, wolves have been hunted for centuries in temperate grasslands because they kill farm animals. Now they are an endangered species.

Hunters often shoot wolves that threaten livestock.

We're in the chain!

Many burgers contain beef from cattle living on what were once wild grassland areas.

Dustbowl danger

If grass is destroyed, either by overgrazing or to grow other crops, this can have a major effect on the land. Thickly matted grass roots just below the ground hold the soil together. One single grass plant may have a network of roots that together measure 4.8 km long! Without the roots, the wind can blow the surface of the soil away and, without proper management, the land may quickly turn into an arid desert. This is increasingly happening in areas such as the steppe.

Food web

Here is an example of who eats who in an African grasslands food web. Surrounding it are some fascinating grasslands facts.

Grasslands are found on every continent of the world except Antarctica.

Lions are only successful in 20-30% of their attempts to hunt prey.

Plants, such as grasses

Decomposers (bacteria and insects that break down dead matter)

Plant-eating insects, such as termites, ants and grasshoppers

Female lions normally do the hunting, but the male lions eat first.

Small rodents, such as mice

Vultures can see prey up to 6.5 km away.

The American prairie was once home to about thirty million bison before they were hunted almost to extinction.

Grass-grazers such
as impala, wildebeest
and gazelles

Big cats, such as lions
and cheetahs

Small predators, such
as mongoose.
Hunts small animals
such as mice

Hyenas and wild dogs

Insect-predators such
as aardvarks and birds

Predatory birds

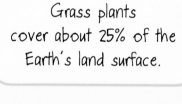

A leopard can carry
prey up to three times its
own body weight up a
tree to hide it from
other hungry grassland
predators.

Grass plants
cover about 25% of the
Earth's land surface.

Rice, eaten the
world over, is a type
of grass plant.

Impala can
bound as far as
14 m and up to 3 m
high. When attacked by
predators, impala bound
in all directions,
confusing the hunters.

Much of the farmland
in southern Canada and the
USA was once grasslands.

Glossary

bird of prey

a bird that hunts and kills other animals for food.

carcass

the dead body of an animal.

carnivore

an animal that eats meat.

chlorophyll

the chemical in plants that gives them their green colour and which captures the sun's energy to make food.

climate

the general weather conditions in a particular area.

cud

partly digested grass brought back into a ruminant's mouth from its first stomach to be chewed again.

equator

an imaginary line that runs around the middle of the Earth dividing it into north and south.

food chain

the feeding links between plants and animals showing who eats whom.

food web

a map of all the feeding links in a habitat showing how the plants and animals are connected to each other.

herbivore

an animal that eats only plants.

hibernation

a way by which some animals survive in winter by dropping into a sleep-like state until spring.

llanos

an area of tropical grassland situated north of the Brazilian rainforest.

micro-organism

a tiny, one-celled life form, such as a bacterium.

migration

the seasonal journey of an animal between one area and another.

omnivore

an animal that eats both plants and meat.

pampas

an area of temperate grassland in southern South America.

prairie

an area of temperate grassland in North America.

predator

an animal that hunts and kills other animals.

photosynthesis

the process by which plants capture the energy of sunlight to make sugar into food.

pride

the name for a large family group of lions.

ruminant

an animal that chews the cud and has a four-part stomach.

savanna

an area of tropical grassland in east Africa.

scavenger

an animal that feeds off the remains of dead creatures and plants.

steppe

an area of temperate grassland stretching from eastern Europe to Mongolia.

temperate grassland

an area of grassland that has four seasons, including a warm summer and a cold winter.

top predator

the animal at the top of a food chain, which no other animal will kill to eat.

tropical grassland

a warm area of grassland, growing near the Equator, with wet and dry seasons.

Grasslands Websites

www.mobot.org/sets/grasslnd/animals/
Information about different kinds of grassland.

www.worldbiomes.com
Find out the different natural areas of the world, including grasslands.

www.bbc.co.uk/nature/wildfacts/
Search out facts about your favourite grassland animals.

www.africam.com
Watch live footage from South Africa's Kruger National Park, and check out amazing camera shots caught on previous days and nights.

www.yahooligans.com
Use this great kids' search engine to find grassland weblinks, via the science and nature category.

Index